Let's Celebrate Series

More Than Matzah

A Passover Feast of Fun, Facts, and Activities

Story by Debbie Herman
Activities by Ann D. Koffsky
Illustrated by Nancy Lane

BARRON'S

I will always remember the wonderful seders of my childhood,
led by my dear father, Melvin Herman Z" L. This book is for him.
-D.H.

To my Mom and Dad, who make wonderful sedarim.
-A.K.

All inquiries should be addressed to:
Barron's Educational Series, Inc.
250 Wireless Boulevard
Hauppauge, New York 11788
http://www.barronseduc.com

ISBN-13: 978-0-7641-3318-3
ISBN-10: 0-7641-3318-7

Library of Congress Catalog Card No. 2005057024

Library of Congress Cataloging-in-Publication Data

Herman, Debbie.
  More than Matzah : a Passover feast of fun, facts, and activities / story by Debbie Herman ;
activities by Ann D. Koffsky ; illustrated by Nancy Lane.
    p. cm. — (Let's celebrate series)
  ISBN-13: 978-0-7641-3318-3
  ISBN-10: 0-7641-3318-7
    1. Passover—Juvenile literature. 2. Seder—Juvenile literature. I. Koffsky, Ann D.
II. Lane, Nancy. III. Title. IV. Series.

BM695.P3H38 2006
296.4'37—dc22

2005057024

Printed in China

9 8 7 6 5 4 3 2 1

Contents

The Story of Passover

Each spring, beginning on the 15th day of the Hebrew month of Nisan, Jews around the world celebrate the holiday of Passover. They set the table with special foods and symbols. They read from a book called the Haggadah. And they retell a story that happened over 3,000 years ago. This story, often called the Exodus, is one of faith, hope, and freedom.

EXTRA INFO

The story of Passover is told in *Exodus*, the second book of the *Bible*. "Exodus" means the departure, or going out, of a large group of people.

The hot rays of the Egyptian sun beat down on the Israelite slaves. As they mixed the mud and straw to make bricks for the Egyptian cities, the taskmasters beat and whipped them.

"Faster! Faster! More straw! More bricks!"

Day in and day out they hauled and dragged and carried. They were tired and weak, and cried out to their God.

FUN FACTS

The houses in ancient Egypt were made out of sun-baked bricks. They were a mixture of mud from the Nile River, straw, and pebbles. This mixture was poured into wooden molds, and left in the sun to dry and harden.

FUN FACTS

Many people think the Israelites built the pyramids, but most scholars believe this is incorrect. According to their estimations, by the time the Israelites became enslaved, the Pyramid Age had long drawn to a close.

But the Israelites had not always been slaves. Their ancestors had once lived freely in the land of Egypt. They had come to Egypt to escape hunger, when famine had swept across their own land, Canaan. The Egyptian king, the pharaoh, had welcomed the Israelites into his country. He allowed them to work as shepherds and worship their one God.

Years passed, and a new king came to power. This pharaoh was suspicious of the Israelites. By now there were very many of them in the land.

EXTRA INFO

Seventy people made the journey from Canaan to Egypt. They were members of one large family. The head of the family was the Jewish forefather, Jacob, also called Israel. His family became known as the Israelites. One of Jacob's sons, Joseph, was already living in Egypt. He was second in command to the pharaoh. So when Joseph's family came to Egypt, the pharaoh welcomed them with open arms. The story of Joseph is found in the *Bible* at the end of the book of *Genesis*.

"The Israelites are numerous and powerful," he told his people. "What if they join our enemies and turn against us?" To weaken the Israelites, he forced them into slavery. So here they were, laboring from dawn to dusk, and wishing to be free.

But still the pharaoh worried. He called to the Israelite midwives - the women who helped deliver the Israelite babies. He told them to kill the newborn males as they were being born. But the midwives refused to listen to the king's command, and the Israelites continued to grow.

"Why have you let the children live?" demanded the pharaoh.

The midwives quickly thought of an excuse. "The Israelite women are not like the Egyptian women. They give birth to their children quickly and easily, without any help. By the time we arrive, the children are already born."

So the pharaoh sent out another order. This one was to the entire nation. They were to drown all newborn Israelite males in the river.

FUN FACTS

Many scholars believe the pharaoh of the *Exodus* was Ramses II, who lived around 1290 – 1224 B.C.E.

One day, an Israelite woman named Jochebed gave birth to a baby boy. She knew her son would be killed, so she put him in a reed basket and sent him down the Nile River. She hoped someone would find her baby, and take care of him. And that's exactly what happened.

The pharaoh's daughter was bathing in the Nile, when she saw a basket hidden among the reeds. Inside the basket was a baby.

"He must be one of the Israelite boys," the princess told her maidservant. "I will raise him as my very own son."

FUN FACTS
Papyrus was a reed that grew in the Nile. Egyptians used it to make baskets, boats, and sandals.

EXTRA INFO
While the *Bible* doesn't give the name of the pharaoh's daughter, *Bible* commentators say it was Bithia.

The baby's sister, Miriam, had been watching from behind some tall grasses. Now she came forward.

"Shall I call an Israelite woman to nurse him?" she asked.

"Yes," said the pharaoh's daughter. And Miriam went to fetch the baby's own mother, Jochebed.

"Take him with you," the princess told Jochebed. "And when he has finished nursing, bring him back to me."

Jochebed did as she was told. She took the baby home, and when he grew older, she brought him back to the princess. The pharaoh's daughter called the boy Moses, an Egyptian word meaning "I drew him out of the water." She raised him in the palace, as her own son. But Moses never forgot he was an Israelite.

EXTRA INFO
The baby also had a brother, Aaron, who would one day help him free the Israelites from slavery.

One day, when Moses was grown, he went out to his people and watched them labor in the heat. As he looked around, he saw an Egyptian beating an Israelite. Moses had to stop him. He hit the Egyptian, and the Egyptian died.

When the pharaoh found out, he ordered Moses killed. Moses fled to the land of Midian, where he lived for many years as a shepherd.

Moses was grazing his sheep one day, when he saw a curious site. A thorn bush was on fire, but it was not burning up. Then, from the bush, came a voice. It was the voice of God.

"Moses, Moses," God called. "I have seen the suffering of my people in Egypt, and I have heard their cries. I will save them from the hands of Egypt, and I will bring them to a land flowing with milk and honey." This was the land of Canaan – the land that would later become known as Israel.

God told Moses to go to the pharaoh and tell him to let the Israelites out of Egypt.

"Who am I to go to the pharaoh?" asked Moses, afraid the king wouldn't listen to him.

"I will be with you," God assured him.

"But I am not a man of words," Moses protested.

"I will tell you what to say," said God. God told Moses to take his brother Aaron with him. Aaron would help him speak to the king. God also told Moses to take his shepherd's staff. With this staff, he would perform miracles.

Moses journeyed back to Egypt, and he and Aaron approached the pharaoh.

"So says the God of Israel: 'Send out my people so that they may worship me in the desert.'"

"Who is this God of yours?" asked the pharaoh, "that I should listen to him?" And instead of freeing the Israelites, he made them work even harder.

"If you do not let the Israelites go," Moses and Aaron warned him, "God will turn the waters of Egypt to blood." But the pharaoh still refused.

So God sent a plague of blood. All the rivers, canals, and ponds of Egypt turned to blood. The fish that had been swimming in them died. And when the people went to drink water, they found blood in their cups and vessels. The plague lasted for seven days, until God turned the blood back to water.

Moses and Aaron returned to the pharaoh. "Let the Israelites go," they warned him, or God would send a plague of frogs. But the pharaoh would not listen. So God sent frogs to cover the land. They were everywhere—in the Egyptians' houses, in their ovens, and even in their beds.

"Remove the frogs and I will free the Israelites," said the pharaoh. God listened to the pharaoh's request, but once the frogs were gone the pharaoh changed his mind.

So God turned the dust of the earth to lice. The Egyptians were covered from head to toe with itchy lice. Their animals were covered too. But the pharaoh still refused to let the Israelites go.

FUN FACTS

Locusts are the world's most destructive insects. A swarm of locusts can destroy 20,000 tons of crops a day.

God sent another plague and another. Wild animals stampeded across the land. The Egyptians' cattle became sick and died. Painful boils covered the Egyptians' bodies. There was destructive hail and swarms of locusts. And when Moses stretched out his staff toward the heavens, God sent a pitch-black darkness. After each plague Moses gave the pharaoh a chance to let the Israelites leave and warned him that another plague would come if he didn't. But each time the pharaoh refused.

Then came the tenth and most terrible plague of all—the death of every Egyptian firstborn son.

At midnight all the firstborn of Egypt died, including the pharaoh's own son. The king ran out into the darkness, in search of Moses and Aaron.

"Rise up!" he told them angrily, "and go out from among my people!"

EXTRA INFO

During the plague of the firstborn, the angel of death passed over the houses of the Israelites so they would not be killed. This is how the holiday became known as Passover.

EXTRA INFO

At the seder there is a custom to spill out a drop of wine from our wine cups as we mention each plague. This reminds us that we should never rejoice over the downfall of our enemies. Even though the Jewish people are happy to be free, they are sad that others had to suffer.

And so, with Moses leading the way, the Israelites fled Egypt. They left so quickly there was no time to prepare food for the journey. They grabbed their bread dough before it had a chance to rise. Moses led the Israelites out of Egypt, into the desert, toward the Red Sea. A column of fire showed them the way to go at night, and a cloud guided them during the day.

FUN FACTS

The invention of bread is attributed to the Egyptians. It seems they discovered fermentation—a process that causes dough to rise. The British Museum has an actual loaf of bread from Ancient Egypt. It is over 3,000 years old.

EXTRA INFO

When the Israelites later baked their un-risen dough, it became matzah, a flat bread made out of flour and water. To remember this, we eat matzah on Passover. Many cities have matzah factories, where you can watch matzah being made by hand.

Back in Egypt, the pharaoh and his people regretted what they had done.

"Why did we let them go?" they asked one another, and they set out after the Israelites in their chariots. Before long, the Egyptians caught up to them.

The Israelites were terrified. The Red Sea was in front of them and the Egyptians were behind them. What were they to do?

"Do not fear!" Moses told his people. "You will see how God will save you!"

At God's command Moses lifted his staff, and stretched it over the sea. Miraculously, the sea split in two. The water stood up like a wall on the right and on the left, with dry land in between. The Israelites ran across the dry land, until they reached the shore.

The Egyptians chased after them, following right behind.

"Stretch your hand over the sea," God told Moses again. And when he did, the waters rushed back in place, drowning the Egyptians.

FUN FACTS

The correct name for the body of water the Israelites crossed is not actually the "Red Sea," but the "Reed Sea." The *Bible* calls the sea by the Hebrew name Yam Suf, meaning "Sea of Reeds."

The Israelites stood at the edge of the sea and looked back in awe and wonder. They sang a song of praise to God, and Miriam led the women in song and dance. They were saved. They were free.

But the story doesn't end here. It only begins. Now the Israelites would embark on a journey through the desert, where they would receive God's Torah—his teachings—and become a nation. This forty-year journey would lead them back to the home of their ancestors—the land of Canaan.

FUN FACTS

In 1776 Thomas Jefferson, Benjamin Franklin, and John Adams suggested a design for the Great Seal of the United States: the image of Moses leading the Israelites through the Red Sea. Their suggestion was not accepted. Instead, the picture of an Egyptian pyramid was used. You can still see it today, on the back of a dollar bill.

Activity Section

by Ann D. Koffsky

A note to kids and their parents: Many of these crafts involve materials that should only be handled with adult supervision. This includes scissors and especially cooking utensils. Please exercise caution, and make this Passover a happy and a safe holiday! Each activity has a *Haggadah* next to its name. The more *Haggadah's* pictured, the more complex the activity (1 is easiest, 4 is hardest).

The Passover meal is the focus of the holiday. It is called a Seder, which in Hebrew means "order." At the Seder meal, many foods and activities are all done in a specific order. The *Haggadah* is the book that helps everyone follow along at the Seder. It has the words to all the songs and the stories to read. It says when to eat each of the special foods, and when to drink the four cups of wine or grape juice. You can buy a *Haggadah* at a bookstore, at many grocery stores, or at a Judaica shop.

Fun Idea—The *Haggadah*

You can make your own Haggadah special by making and decorating a book cover and book mark for it. You can also write, "This Haggadah belongs to…" on a computer label, and stick it inside the front cover.

Seder Clock

This Seder-clock decoration will help everyone at the table keep track of what part their Seder is up to.

You will need:
1 sheet of white poster board
1 sheet of black poster board
1 paper fastener

Scissors
Pencil
Ruler
Black marker

Crayon
Yarn
Masking tape

1. Cut out a giant circle from your poster board.

2. Using a pencil and a ruler, divide the circle into fourteen parts as shown below.

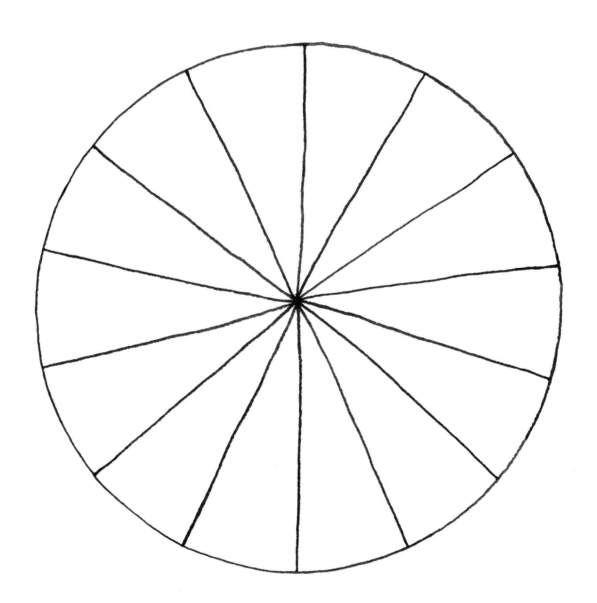

3. Use the black marker to write the names of each of the 14 Seder parts around the circle as illustrated below. Write one name in each section. You can also draw your own pictures about the parts of the Seder next to its name. Be sure to keep them in order!

4. Color each of the sections in with colored crayons (the black marker will show through). Make sure that each section is a different color.

5. Use a pencil to punch a hole through the middle of the circle.

6. Cut out a giant arrow from the black poster board. Punch a hole through the bottom of the arrow.

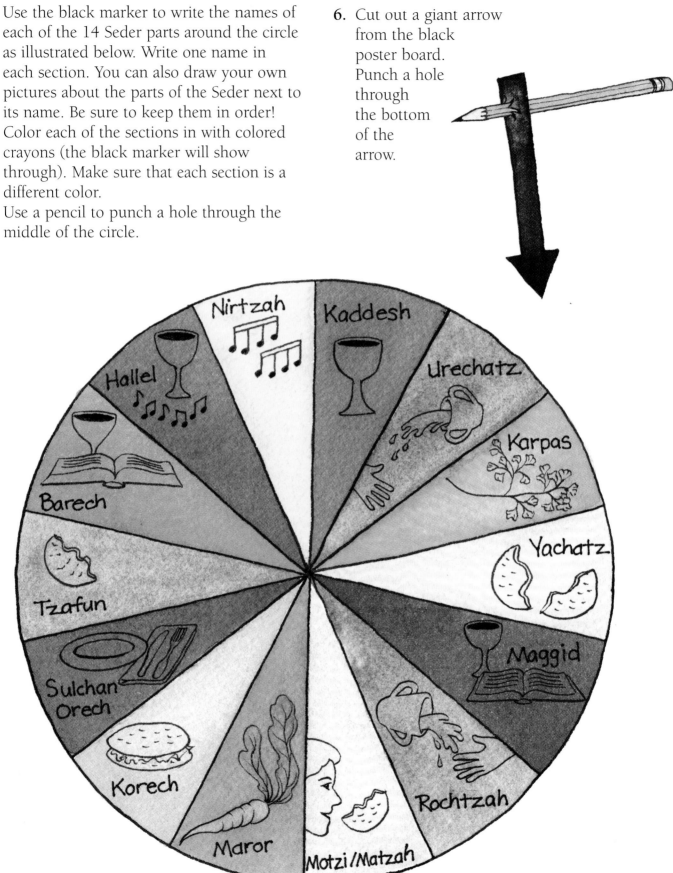

7. Thread the paper fastener through the two punched holes, and attach the arrow to the circle.

8. Tape two ends of a piece of yarn to the back of the circle.

9. Hang your Seder clock in a place where everyone can see it. During the Seder, point the arrow around the clock as you get to each part.

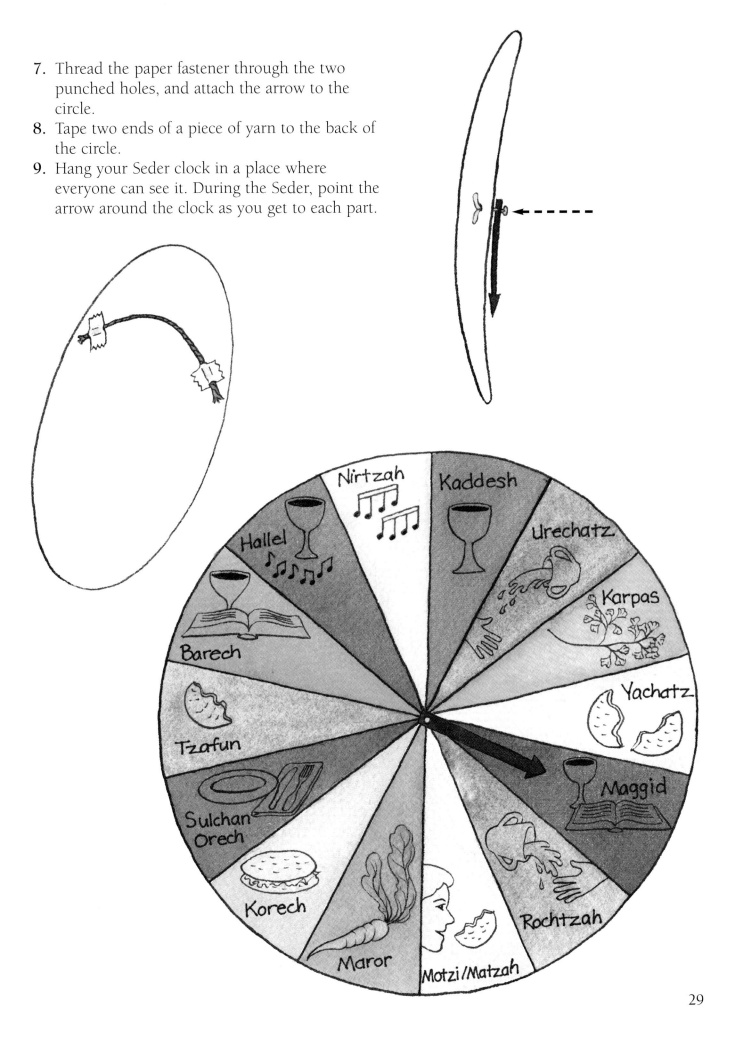

Make a Seder Plate / Matzah Holder

The Seder plate holds some of the symbolic Seder foods. Many Seder plates are also designed to hold the three main matzahs that the leader uses.
To make this kind of Seder plate, you will need:

1 egg carton
4 octagon, 10-inch paper dinner plates
Glue

6 solo/condiment cups (these are the little plastic cups that some take-out restaurants put salad dressing in)

Paint
Construction paper: green, brown, white, and purple

1. Cut out nine of the egg holders from the egg carton, and trim the edges

2. Glue three of the egg holders onto the first paper plate, as shown

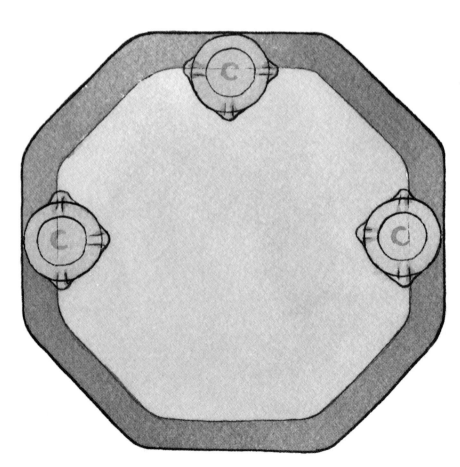

3. Glue three more egg holders onto the second paper plate, and the last three onto the third paper plate.

4. Take one of the condiment cups and trace its bottom onto a piece of white construction paper. Draw an egg in that circle, and cut it out. Do the same for the other Seder plate foods: Cut the shank bone out of a brown circle, parsley and lettuce from green circles, charoset from a purple circle, and maror from a white circle.

5. Glue the pictures of the Seder foods onto the right spots of the fourth plate (see picture).

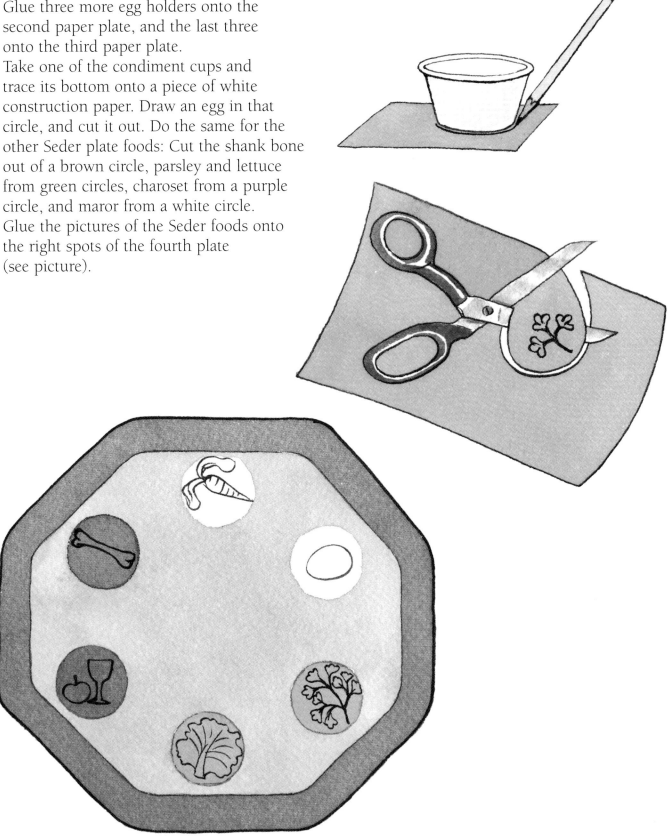

6. Glue the bottom of a condiment cup over each food picture on the plate.
7. Put a generous amount of glue onto the top of each egg holder, and stack the next plate on top. Repeat for the remaining plates. Glue the plate with the food pictures on the top.
8. To use at your Seder meal, place one matzah on each of the bottom three plates. Then, fill your plate's cups with the following foods:

Baytzah / Egg

The egg is a symbol of birth, and it reminds us that on Passover the Jewish nation was born. Since it is also a reminder of the holiday sacrifice that was brought in the ancient temple for holidays, we burn a spot on its shell.

Charoset

The charoset is thick and mushy: just like the cement the Jewish slaves were forced to mix. Jews from different parts of the world have different recipes for Charoset. Here are two:

Sephardic (Middle Eastern, Spanish) style recipe
1/2 cup dates, chopped
1 cup apples, chopped
1/2 cup walnuts, chopped
1/2 cup almonds, chopped
1/8 teaspoon pepper
1 teaspoon cinnamon
2 tablespoons sweet red wine

Combine all ingredients and refrigerate.

Ashkenazik (German, Polish, Russian) style recipe
2 cups apples
2 cups chopped walnuts
2 teaspoons cinnamon
2 tablespoons sweet red wine

Combine all ingredients and refrigerate.

Z'roah / Shank Bone

At that first Passover celebrated in Egypt, the Jewish people ate a roasted lamb with their dinner. The Seder plate includes a roasted shank bone as a reminder.

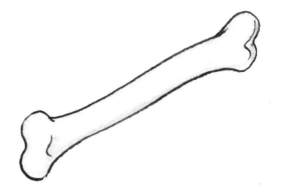

Karpas / Parsley and Chazeret / Lettuce

Both of these foods are on the plate because Passover is a Springtime holiday. At the beginning of the Seder meal, the Karpas is dipped into salty water, just like the salty tears of the Jewish slaves.

Marror/ Bitter Herb

The bitter herb is eaten to remind those at the Seder of the bitterness of slavery. Different families use different vegetables for the Marror, like Horseradish, Romaine lettuce, or endives.

Mosaic Matzah Container

Hardboiled eggs are often served at Seder meals.
Here is a project that finds a great use for all those egg shells!

You will need:
An 11-inch square of Bristol
  paper or poster board

Scissors
White glue
12 Hardboiled eggs

White vinegar
Food coloring,
  assorted colors
1 Egg carton

To make the matzah holder:

1. Fold up the sides of the 11-inch square to create a 1 1/2-inch border.
   Then open the square again and lay it flat.

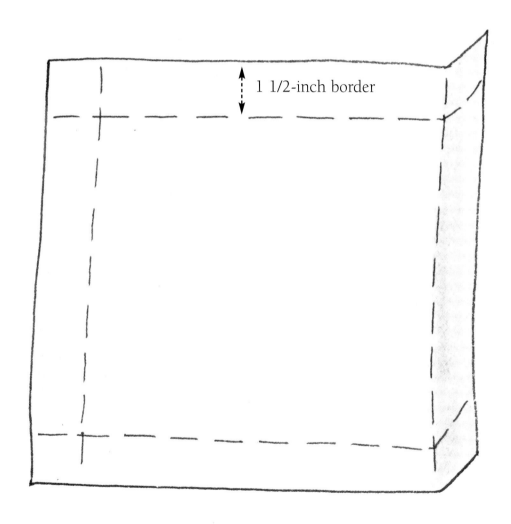

1 1/2-inch border

2. At each corner, cut one slit as shown in the picture.

3. Fold the borders in again, and overlap the corners. Glue each corner in place to form a box.

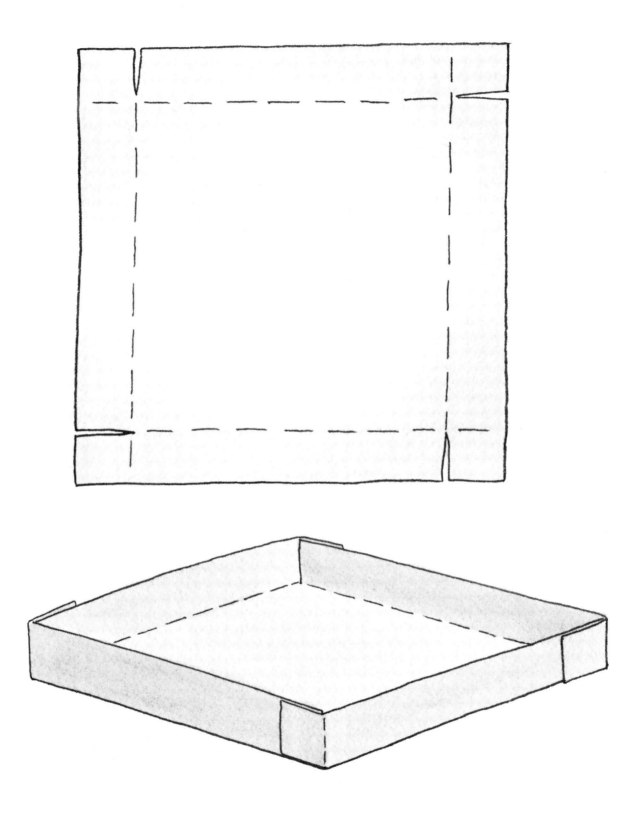

To create the egg dye mixtures:

1. Put about 20 drops of food coloring into a cup or bowl.
2. Add 1 teaspoon of white vinegar to the cup.
3. Ask a grown-up to help you fill each cup with a 1/2 cup of boiling water.
4. Stir. Repeat these steps for each color you want to make.
5. Gently drop your cooled, hardboiled eggs into each cup of dye. They should stay there for about 5 minutes.
6. Remove the eggs from the dye, and put them into the egg carton to dry.
7. Once the eggs are all dry, peel the shells off. Be sure to peel off the thin papery part too.
   This will help the shells stick better later.

8. Decorate your matzah holder with the shells by putting glue onto the outsides of the box, and placing the shells on top. You can make stripes, squares, or a pretty pattern. You could copy the Hebrew words for "Passover" and "matzah" shown on this page onto one of the sides, too.

9. Once it is all dry, put your matzahs inside, and add the holder to your Seder table.

*Note: Dying the eggshells does not affect the color or taste of the actual egg inside, so you can still serve and eat them on Passover.

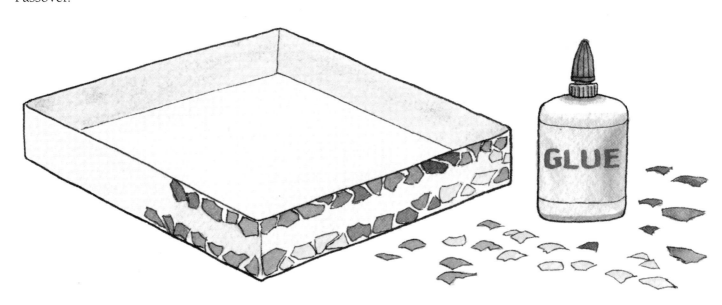

Fun Idea

If you have leftover eggshells, you can make a matching salt-water dish. Just glue the shells to a plastic bowl. When you're done, fill the bowl with water and a little bit of salt, and put it next to the Seder plate on your table.

Haggadah Songs

Try singing this song as a game. Going around the table, have each player sing a paragraph without taking a breath. This gets harder as the paragraphs get longer.

Who Knows One?

Who knows one? I know one! One is our God in heaven and earth.

Who knows two? I know two! Two are the tablets of the covenant; One is our God in heaven and earth.

Who knows three? I know three! Three are the fathers of Israel; Two are the tablets of the covenant; One is our God in heaven and earth.

Who knows four? I know four! Four are the mothers of Israel; Three are the fathers of Israel; Two are the tablets of the covenant; One is our God in heaven and earth.

Who knows five? I know five! Five are the books of the *Torah*; Four are the mothers of Israel; Three are the fathers of Israel; Two are the tablets of the covenant; One is our God in heaven and earth.

Who knows six? I know six! Six are the orders of the Mishnah; Five are the books of the *Torah*; Four are the mothers of Israel; Three are the fathers of Israel; Two are the tablets of the covenant; One is our God in heaven and earth.

Who knows seven? I know seven! Seven are the days of the week; Six are the orders of the Mishnah; Five are the books of the *Torah*; Four are the mothers of Israel; Three are the fathers of Israel; Two are the tablets of the covenant; One is our God in heaven and earth.

Who knows eight? I know eight! Eight are the days to circumcision; Seven are the days of the week; Six are the orders of the Mishnah; Five are the books of the *Torah*; Four are the mothers of Israel; Three are the fathers of Israel; Two are the tablets of the covenant; One is our God in heaven and earth.

Who knows nine? I know nine! Nine are the months to childbirth; Eight are the days to circumcision; Seven are the days of the week; Six are the orders of the Mishnah; Five are the books of the *Torah*; Four are the mothers of Israel; Three are the fathers of Israel; Two are the tablets of the covenant; One is our God in heaven and earth.

Who knows ten? I know ten! Ten are the commandments; Nine are the months to childbirth; Eight are the days to circumcision; Seven are the days of the week; Six are the orders of the Mishnah; Five are the books of the *Torah*; Four are the mothers of Israel; Three are the fathers of Israel; Two are the tablets of the covenant; One is our God in heaven and earth.

Who knows eleven? I know eleven! Eleven are the stars in Joseph's dream; Ten are the commandments; Nine are the months to childbirth; Eight are the days to circumcision; Seven are the days of the week; Six are the orders of the Mishnah; Five are the books of the *Torah*; Four are the mothers of Israel; Three are the fathers of Israel; Two are the tablets of the covenant; One is our God in heaven and earth.

Who knows twelve? I know twelve! Twelve are the tribes of Israel; Eleven are the stars in Joseph's dream; Ten are the commandments; Nine are the months to childbirth; Eight are the days to circumcision; Seven are the days of the week; Six are the orders of the Mishnah; Five are the books of the *Torah*; Four are the mothers of Israel; Three are the fathers of Israel; Two are the tablets of the covenant; One is our God in heaven and earth.

Who knows thirteen? I know thirteen! Thirteen are the attributes of God; Twelve are the tribes of Israel; Eleven are the stars in Joseph's dream; Ten are the commandments; Nine are the months to childbirth; Eight are the days to circumcision; Seven are the days of the week; Six are the orders of the Mishnah; Five are the books of the *Torah*; Four are the mothers of Israel; Three are the fathers of Israel; Two are the tablets of the covenant; One is our God in heaven and earth.

Chad Gadya

One little goat, one little goat,
   that Father bought for two coins.
One little goat, one little goat.

Then came the cat and ate the goat,
   that Father bought for two coins.
One little goat, one little goat.

Then came the dog and bit the cat
   that ate the goat,
   that Father bought for two coins.
One little goat, one little goat.

Then came the stick and beat the dog
   that bit the cat that ate the goat,
   that Father bought for two coins.
One little goat, one little goat.

Then came fire and burned the stick
   that beat the dog that bit the cat
   that ate the goat,
   that Father bought for two coins.
One little goat, one little goat.

Then came the water and quenched
   the fire that burned the stick that
   beat the dog that bit the cat that ate
   the goat,
   that Father bought for two coins.
One little goat, one little goat.

Then came the ox and drank the water
   that quenched the fire that burned
   the stick that beat the dog that bit
   the cat that ate the goat,
   that Father bought for two coins.
One little goat, one little goat.

Then came the butcher and
   slaughtered the ox that drank the
   water that quenched the fire that
   burned the stick that beat the dog
   that bit the cat that ate the goat,
   that Father bought for two coins.
One little goat, one little goat.

Then came the angel of death and
   killed the butcher who slaughtered
   the ox that drank the water that
   quenched the fire that burned the
   stick that beat the dog that bit the
   cat that ate the goat,
   that Father bought for two coins.
One little goat, one little goat.

Then came the Holy One, blessed be
   He, and slew the angel of death that
   killed the butcher who slaughtered
   the ox that drank the water that
   quenched the fire that burned the
   stick that beat the dog that bit the
   cat that ate the goat,
   that Father bought for two coins.
One little goat, one little goat.

The Four Questions

Many things at the Seder were designed to get children curious, so that they would ask, "Why are we doing this?" and become involved. The "Four Questions" listed in the Haggadah *are meant to be just the beginning of the childrens' questions. In many families, it is the job of the youngest child to ask them. They are:*

How is this night different from all other nights?

On all other nights we eat bread or matzah, but tonight we eat only matzah?

On all other nights we don't even dip our vegetables one time, but tonight we dip twice?

On all other nights we eat all kinds of vegetables, but tonight we eat marror?

On all other nights we eat sitting straight, or reclining, but tonight we all recline?

You Did It! 4 Questions Award

Saying those questions can be tough, so you should get an award!

You will need:
One plastic can lid of any size (the top of a coffee can works well)
Markers
Glitter
Ribbon
Glue
1 sheet of construction paper
Safety pin
Scissors

1. Using your can lid, trace a circle onto your construction paper. Cut out the circle.

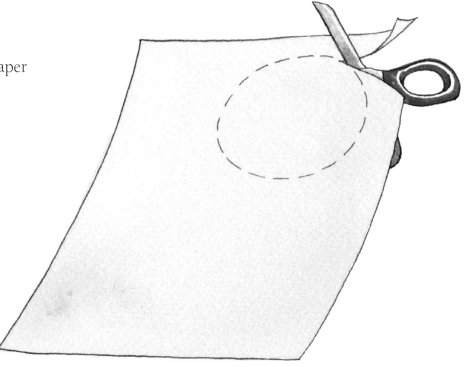

2. Write, "I said the four questions!" onto the circle, and decorate with your markers and glitter.

3. Glue the circle onto the can lid.

4. Fold your ribbon in half, so that it looks like a "V."

5. Glue the bottom of the "V" to the back of the can lid. Glue the ribbon pieces together so that it will stay in the "V" shape.

6. Have a grown-up thread the safety pin through the ribbon. After you say the four questions, have a grown-up pin the award to your shirt. Well done!

Fun Idea

Don't stop with the 4 questions! Keep asking! Play stump your parents. Take turns asking the grown-ups questions about the Seder. Whoever asks a question the grown-up can't answer gets a point. Keep score by giving a nut or candy for each point earned. The person with the most points at the end wins.

Pin the Plagues on Pharaoh!

To play "Pin the Plagues," first make a "Wanted!" poster of the pharaoh.

You will need:
A poster board
Markers
Scissors

1. Draw a large rectangle in the middle of the poster board. Inside the rectangle, draw a picture of an Egyptian pharaoh. You can copy the one we've drawn on this page.
2. Write "**WANTED!**" over the picture
3. Write these sentences under the rectangle:

"Pharaoh, The new ruler of Egypt
A.K.A. Ramses II.
For enslaving the Jewish Nation!
Jews must be freed, or plagues WILL come!
If you have information that might lead to freedom for the Jewish slaves,
contact Moses, Aaron, or Miriam."

4. Cut out ten rectangles from another sheet of poster board.

5. On each of the rectangles, write the names of one of the plagues: Blood, Frogs, Lice, Pestilence, Cattle Sickness, Boil, Hail, Locusts, Darkness, Slaying of the Firstborn. You can also draw pictures of each of the plagues.

6. Attach masking tape to each plague and play "Pin the Plagues" the same way as you would "Pin the Tail on the Donkey."

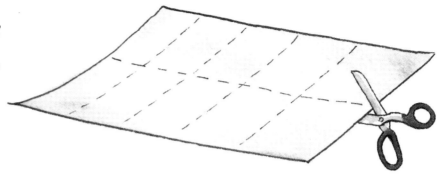

The Four Sons Puppet

The Haggadah discusses the four different types of children who are at the Seder table: the wise child, the simple child, the rebellious child, and the child who does not know how to ask. To make a puppet of the four children, you will need:

Two empty toilet paper rolls   Ruler
Scissors   Glue
Construction paper   Markers
Pencil

1. Cut one toilet tube into 3 pieces. Make the first cut in the middle of the tube, and then cut one part in half again. The big part of the tube will be the bodies, and the other parts will be the faces and hair.

2. Cover each section of tube with a different colored strip of construction paper. To see how wide your strip should be, lay the tube down on its side at the edge of the paper and make a pencil mark on the paper at the edge of the tube. This is how wide your strip should be.

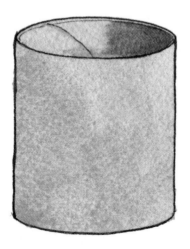

3. Flatten the second toilet tube, and fold it along the middle, lengthwise.

4. Push the flat tube through the inside of each of the paper covered tubes, so that the hair section is on top, the face section is in the middle, and the body section is on the bottom.

5. When all the pieces are on, poke your finger inside the flat tube and open it out again as far as it will go. It will still be a little squashed, but that's OK.

6. Wih a pencil, draw four faces around the middle tube, four hats around the top tube, and four bodies for each of the four children on the big tube. When choosing what to draw for each part, ask yourself these questions: What kind of face do you think the simple child should have? What could a wise child be holding in his hands? What kind of hats should each child wear? After you're done, mix and match their bodies and see what other kinds of questions you can ask about the children. You can also bring the puppet to your Seder, and hold up each child when it's time to read about it.

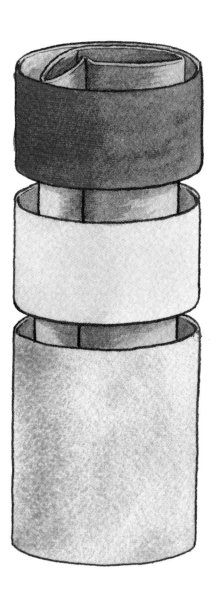

Afikoman Bag

You will need:
A large 10 x 13 envelope   Labels from Passover products
A small piece of Velcro   Glue
                                   Pencil

1. Stick one side of the Velcro to the envelope flap, and one side to the envelope. This way you will be able to open and close the envelope as many times as you'd like.
2. Tear off labels from Passover products, such as a box of matzah, matzah meal, horseradish, grape juice, etc.
3. Make a collage with labels on the envelope.
4. When the time is right, secretly place the afikoman matzah in the envelope, and hide it!

Afikoman Game

"Afikoman" is the name given to half of the middle matzah. It is put away at the beginning of the Seder, and saved for dessert. The Seder cannot end until it is eaten.

In some families, the children sneak the afikoman from the table and hide it away. Knowing that it must be eaten, the grown-ups bargain for its return, offering prizes such as toys or money. Some families ask the children to give a part of their afikoman money to charity.

Other families use the afikoman as the treasure in a treasure hunt. The grown-ups hide the matzah, and all the children look for it. The child who finds the afikoman is the winner.